POLICE ETHICS AND PROFESSIONAL CONDUCT

A Concise Best Practice Guide for Police Officers in African Societies.

DR CHARLES OMOLE

Copyright 2017

By

Charles Omole

ISBN: 978-1-907095-26-9

Published by:

WINNING FAITH

London . New York . Lagos

DEDICATION

This book is dedicated to all Law Enforcement Officers across the continent of Africa.

TABLE OF CONTENTS

CHAPTER ONE .... - 13 -
OVERVIEW OF ETHICS AND PROFESSIONAL
CONDUCT IN POLICING..............................- 13 -
WHAT IS ETHICS ....- 15 -
HISTORICAL OVERVIEW OF ETHICS.....- 17 -
Police Discretionary Powers ....- 24 -
FIVE SPECTRUMS OF ETHICS IN POLICING
....- 30 -

CHAPTER TWO ....- 33 -
WHY DOES ETHICS MATTER? ....- 33 -
ETHICAL BREACHES BY POLICE
OFFICERS ....- 37 -
SUBSTANTIVE v PROCEDURAL JUSTICE ..-
38 -
POLICE STANDARD OF BEHAVIOUR....- 39 -
ETHICS AND POLICING – A BRIEF
HISTORY...- 40 -

CHAPTER THREE.. - 51 -
HOW BAD IS THE PROBLEM OF ETHICS?- 51 -
KEY WEAKNESSES OF POLICE
INSTITUTIONS IN AFRICA.........................- 54 -
PERSONAL ETHICAL EXERCISE-1 ....- 59 -

CHAPTER FOUR .... - 61 -
ETHICAL CATEGORISATION OF POLICE
OFFICERS ....- 61 -
THE BAD CHARACTER...............................- 62 -
THE WEAK CHARACTER ....- 62 -
THE SELF-CONTROLLED CHARACTER- 63 -

THE EXCELLENT CHARACTER................- 64 -
STAGES AND PROGRESSION OF POLICE
ATTITUDES FORMATION DURING THEIR
CAREER..- 65 -
    IDEALISTIC STAGE..- 66 -
    FRUSTRATED STAGE ....- 66 -
    DEFIANT STAGE..- 67 -
    RESIGNED STAGE ....- 67 -
    AWARE STAGE..- 68 -
    DECISIVE STAGE..- 68 -
    COMMITMENT STAGE..- 68 -
    REFELCTION EXERCISES................................- 71 -

CHAPTER FIVE...- 73 -
  THE PATHOLOGY OF ....- 73 -
  POLICE ETHICS ....- 73 -
    TRAINED INCAPACITY.............................- 73 -
    OCCUPATIONAL PSYCHOSIS ....- 74 -
    FUNDAMENTAL AMBIVALENCE..............- 75 -
    SACREDIFICATION...................................- 75 -
    GOAL DISPLACEMENT.............................- 76 -
    ESPIRIT D'CORPS....................................- 76 -
    ORGANISATIONAL ARROGANCE ....- 76 -
    EXPERIENCE v PROCEDURE ....- 77 -

CHAPTER SIX..- 79 -
  POLICE ETHICS AND ACCOUNTABILITY- 79 -

CHAPTER SEVEN ....- 95 -
  WHAT SHAPES THE MINDS OF POLICE
  OFFICERS ....- 95 -
    OBJECTIVE v SUBJECTIVE INFORMATION-
    97 -
    POLICE INFORMATION SOURCES.........- 99 -
    POLICE SUB-CULTURE..........................- 100 -
    SUPERVISION ....- 101 -

CHAPTER EIGHT .... - 105 -
POLICE ETHICAL DECISION-MAKING
FRAMEWORK .... - 105 -
**ESSENTIAL VALUES THAT SHAPES THE
STANDARD OF BEHAVIOUR IN POLICING:** -
106 -
**THE THREE OVERARCHING TEST GUIDE
TO INDIVIDUAL ETHICAL DECISION
MAKING**..- *109* -
CRITICAL THINKING TEST .... - 109 -
THE MEDIA TEST... - 110 -
THE INTUITIVE TEST .... - 110 -
THE MODEL ETHICAL POLICE ORGANISATION. -
111 -
**CHALLENGING AND REPORTING ETHICAL
BREACHES** .... - 118 -
WHISTLEBLOWER POLICY .... - 119 -
ETHICAL CODE FOR EACH NATION....- 119 -
ETHICAL DECISION MODEL................... - 121 -
PERSONAL ETHICAL EXERCISE-2..........**- 127 -**
ETHICAL EXERCISE 2 - ANALYSIS ...... - 128 -

ETHICS SELF-ASSESSMENT EXERCISES.. - 131 -
AN ETHICAL CREED ....**- 135 -**

APPENDIX 1 .... - 137 -
RESOLUTION ON POLICE AND HUMAN RIGHTS IN
AFRICA...**- 137 -**

APPENDIX 2 .... - 141 -
RESOLUTION ON POLICE REFORM, ACCOUNTABILITY
AND CIVILIAN POLICE OVERSIGHT IN AFRICA..**- 141 -**

APPENDIX 3 .... - 145 -
RESOLUTION ON THE NEED TO DEVELOP
GUIDELINES ON POLICING AND ASSEMBLIES IN
AFRICA - ACHPR/RES. 363(LIX) 2016 ....**- 145 -**

APPENDIX 4 .... - 149 -
    LAUNCH OF THE GUIDELINES ON CONDITIONS OF
    ARREST, POLICE CUSTODY AND PRE-TRIAL
    DETENTION IN AFRICA .... - 149 -
    RELATED BOOKS BY DR OMOLE ....- 157 -

INTRODUCTION

Police enjoy widespread powers across the nations, so the cases of countries in Africa is no different. As the tool used by the Executive branch to enforce the law, the police is greatly misunderstood in many African countries and as such not held in high regard and considered an apparatus of the corrupt political governments in power.

Yet the work of the police is governed by laws in all countries. But the issue of ethics in policing has become a major measurement of how effective a police organisation is as it affects the perception of the public in a direct way.

A more ethical police organisation is likely to enjoy greater support from the people than an unethical one. This quest to increase the profile, acceptance and status of police officers in African countries is why I have written this concise book on police ethics in Africa. Just to start the debate and engage policy makers on the need for a code of ethics enshrined in law.

Ethical behaviour comes from the values, beliefs, attitudes and knowledge that guide the judgements of each individual police officer. Everyone in policing has to make difficult decisions and complex choices every day of the week. These range from how to talk to a distressed member of the public through to how to allocate scarce resources or even whether to take a life. These are not easy choices.

There is therefore a need for an ethical blueprint or protocol that will govern and inform all the actions of the police. This will be done in slightly different ways in different countries. But this book will expose the reader to the basic factors that can shape the ethics of police officers and how good practices can be established across the continent.

This is not an exhaustive book on ethics or even ethics in policing. That is why the word "concise" is included in the sub title of the book. Ethics is a wide ranging topic that can be analysed from multiple perspectives. My aim in this book is to give a concise overview of operational ethics for the rank and file to consult from time to time. It is a guide that I hope will soon become indispensable. The book has been written in an accessible format and simple words that will make understanding easier even for the least educated officer.

There are enough materials in this succinct book to incentify reform of policing in Africa, leading to a more detailed and bespoke work by each nation to perfect their police operations in ways that is ethically sound based on African Union's overarching principles of excellence in policing.

This book is written for the serving police officer who daily confronts the ethical dilemmas common to police work. It is in plain English and written in a way to guide your decision making, even if your police organisation lack a corporate ethical code of practice. Hence the book is deliberately condensed to fit into your top drawer.

So congratulations as you are about to be challenged, informed, educated, and inspired all at the same time. A police officer reading this book will enjoy it tremendously and find it practical and easy to read. As a concise book, it is small enough to be completed in a few hours of reading.

This will perhaps be one of the best books on policing you may have read so far. So be the best you can be as a police officer and do your nation proud.

I am over and out.

Sincerely

Dr Charles Omole
2017

CHAPTER ONE

OVERVIEW OF ETHICS AND PROFESSIONAL CONDUCT IN POLICING

There tends to be many misconceptions about ethics whenever police officers hear the word. I will like to start by removing any misconceived ideas about what ethics and profession conduct represent. Why do I need to read or learn about it you may ask?

I am certain by the time you finish this book, it will become abundantly clear why you need to refresh your skill and understanding of ethics and professional conduct. Ethics is not a static skill. It is dynamic.

It needs to reflect the latest consensus or understanding as African societies develop and adopt modern lifestyles and ways of doing things. It is a skill that can easily become outdated if not updated. Ethical conundrums and challenges evolves all the time as society evolve.

And there is no static right or wrong ways of dealing with some difficulties; there exist however a range of acceptable responses which substantially depend on your knowledge, exposure and training.

So you give yourself the best possible chance of making the right decision, when you are fully updated on new developments and thinking in police circles and legal jurisprudence.

Ethics is not indoctrination. The goal isn't to make everyone the same; it is about character and decision-making. Ethics is not an underhanded attempt to change you. No one can change you; you can only change yourself. Ethics is a process of understanding yourself better; why you tend to believe, think and act the way you do.

Ethics is not an assumption that your ethics are flawed. This isn't remedial ethics. This is a book to help basically decent people learn to make the best choices and decisions as they confront the challenges of policing in African societies.

WHAT IS ETHICS

Ethics is a process of understanding yourself better; why you tend to believe, think and act the way you do. Ethics is learning how to choose the wisest course of action in difficult situations.

Ethics is a code of values which guides our choices and actions and determines the purpose and course of our lives. As police officers, ethics is not just about what you do, but also about why you do what you do.

Ethics is vital and necessary to all police functions and activities. It is even more important and indispensable in societies where the police in addition to investigating crimes also initiate legal prosecutions of suspects.

Understanding of ethics can save your career and retirement as a police officer. It can make your job easier. It can help restore public trust in law enforcement.

You also need to be aware that ethics is a perishable skill. It requires continual training and honing, just like driving and shooting. The more updated you are, the better you will be at making ethical decisions as a police officer.

So I will like you to approach this topic and this book with an open mind. You need to take on the mind-set that "I don't know everything yet, and can learn something valuable from reading about the ideas of others." A positive and cooperative attitude is essential.

Understanding the behaviour of the police is one of the most interesting concerns in policing. As police officer, he/she possess authority to enforce the law and the duty to maintain peace and order.

The decisions made by a police officer has a profound impact on the lives of those individuals with whom they interact. This is why ethics is vitally Important in police operations worldwide.

Sustainable ethical behaviour requires moral sensitivity and moral judgement. Moral sensitivity is the the ability to recognise the presence and nature of ethical issues; the awareness that a situation represents an ethical problem that requires an ethical decision.

Moral judgment however, is the ability to make the right ethical decision; to determine the morally correct and wisest course of action. This requires the use of critical thinking skills and the ability to prioritise competing ethical principles and values.

HISTORICAL OVERVIEW OF ETHICS

As a field of study, ethics is a branch of philosophy which studies the principles of right or wrong in human conduct. Right or wrong are qualities assigned to actions, conduct and behaviour. Ethics in Policing deals with Why and How you conduct yourself as Officers.

➢ Right ACTION,
➢ Right CONDUCT,
➢ Right BEHAVIOUR.

We shall be looking at Professional Conduct as it relates to Ethical Behaviour. Modern ethical connection with the law came out of historical Equity and Trust principles.

To understand fully how ethics work within the traditional certainties law enforcement is supposed to provide, we will need to go into a bit of history of how the concept of equity was developed and how it has now become the key basis of legal enforcement of rules in modern and African societies.

"Equity had come not to destroy the law, but to fulfil it" was stated by Frederic William Maitland in Lectures on Equity written in the last century. The quote by Maitland represented his verdict on the tension that

customarily has been seen to exist between Equity and Common Law and his reflection on whether equity evolved out of necessity to perpetuate the smooth operations of the common law for public good or if equity came into existence purely as a challenge to the authority and monopoly of the common law to dispense justice.

The universality of the common law became problematic in the early centuries due to its creation of laws common to all. This means making rules without exceptions and the strict adherence to old legal precedents despite changing societal landscape.

There was also perceived incidents of jury intimidations in common law courts that had the potential to bring the justice system into disrepute. So came equity to the rescue.

The word equity means *fairness or being just*; but in legal terms it can be said to be the rules developed to mitigate the severity or constraints of the common law. As we shall examine later in this book, the concept of *police discretion* came out of equity. This concept allows officers to choose not to enforce the law in special circumstances; if enforcement of the law will not be equitable or just or could bring the police into disrepute.

For instance, a man doing 70mph in a 60mph zone is breaking the law. But when stopped by the police it was discovered that his wife was in labour and about to deliver, so he was running to the hospital.

Does the officer ignore the facts and proceed to give him a speeding ticket and fine; or does he respond to the facts by not only letting him off but possibly helping his get to the hospital as quickly as possible. This is an equitable decision based on the doctrine of discretion that officers have.

Equity developed alongside the common law as a separate legal authority administered by the Court of Chancery in England. The common law was seen as deficient in many ways and many went to the King for redress after common law verdicts that were considered unjust or unfair.

With massive increase in such petitions to the King, the Chancellor (usually a Clergy) was delegated by the King to oversee these petitions. This gradually developed into the Court of Equity.

At the time, the common law had many deficiencies. Firstly, the writ/summons system made any new claim possible only if it is based on an existing writ. And if none exists, then the case would normally not proceed.

This became a big problem as many could not even initiate their petition in the common law courts. Also, there was limitation in the kind of remedies offered by the common law courts.

Damages were the dominant civil remedy available, but this did not satisfy the need for justice by many litigants who would have preferred an injunction or order for specific performance. In addition, the common law courts failed to adequately recognise certain types of rights, such as beneficial owners in a Trust. The use of the Court of Equity (also known as Court of Chancery) to resolve Trust related matters became very popular.

With these deficiencies; there were growing number of unhappy citizens who petitioned the King for justice. These discretionary verdicts by the King's court (and later the Court of Chancery); gave birth to equitable remedies, thus establishing equity as a doctrine in English legal landscape.

In its early days; the Chancellors decided cases without much reference to previously written verdicts. After all, the Chancellors were expected to decide cases based on *morality, fairness and good conscience.*

There were concern that two parallel legal systems have developed in the country; with its attendant conflict of jurisdiction and both vying for superiority. To address this confusion; Then came the Judicature Acts of 1873 and 1875 (JA). The 1873 JA specifically stated that in case where there is conflict between Equity and Common Law rules; Equity should prevail.[1]

The JA also got rid of the old separate courts of common law and equity and in its place established the High Court and the Court of Appeal to adjudicate over both common law and equity matters.

Over time, the JA inspired (together with the body of rules of the court made by judges); the creation of a Code of Civil Procedure which sought to combine the best of both common law and equity systems. This reduced significantly any obvious perception of conflict between the two systems. *'Equity follows the law'* is a common maxim in equity jurisprudence.

This means that equity follows all the dictates of the common law and will only step in if after all have been done, something was still needed to satisfy justness and equity. This is

---

[1] Section 44 of the Law and Equity Act codifies the principle of the Earl of Oxford (1644) case: if rules of equity and law conflict, equity prevails.

the basis of the quote by Maitland that "Equity had come not to destroy the law, but to fulfil it".

So equity can be said to complement the law. And with the fusion of the courts by the JA, it became possible to obtain both legal and equitable remedies from the same court. Hence equity has become like an appendix to common law intended to achieve fairness and justice (after all the rules of common law has been applied and fulfilled). This equitable concept gives the police powers and discretion on how to enforce a given law.

Police Discretionary Powers

Police Discretion is the inherent ability and privilege of a police officer to test and use the limits of his power in making a choice among possible courses of action or inaction (i.e. to arrest or not to arrest).

A police officer could ignore an infringement of the law, he could give verbal or written warning, or he could arrest and prosecute. The officer's response will depend upon the facts of the situation.

But this discretionary police powers (created by equity and intended to smooth the rough edges of statutes law) can easily be abused by corrupt officers. However, discretion can only be correctly interpreted as those decisions that are made with lawful authority rather than decisions made for illegal reasons. This is where good ethical knowledge comes in to aid the proper response of the officer in situations like this.

The police are not alone in being given the power to vary application of common law to fit individual peculiar facts in order to achieve fairness. In the criminal justice landscape, Equity in its self-adaptive best have continued to endure through devise of new equitable principles such as the MAREVA[2] injunction and ANTO PILLAR[3] orders.

These self-adaptive characteristics has sometimes been captured by the modern term Unconscionability. Equitable remedies are

---

[2] Mareva v International Bulkcarriers [1975] 2 Lloyd's Rep 509
[3] Anton Piller v Manufacturing Processes Ltd [1976] Ch 55

discretionary even till today; whereas legal remedies are as of right. This makes equitable outcome less fully predictable compared to common law outcomes.

Equity's ability to innovate has always been demonstrated as evident in many cases where the court has been able to refine, adapt and differentiate the application of many long-standing equitable maxims, as it has always done.

It may be argued that equity's focus on individual justice creates a conflict with the common law's focus on universal justice. For instance, the maxim that *'equity will not allow a statute to be used as cloak for fraud'* has the result of preventing reliance on statutory and common law if the outcome will be unconscionable.

This may be seen as a licence from equity to ignore the common law; Thus delivering individual personal and fair outcomes[4] that

---

[4] Dillwyn v Llewelyn (1862) 45 E.R. 1285

can vary from case to case (regardless of similar facts); instead of the universal outcome of the common law. This is what the police discretionary power is supposed to achieve; fairness.

the court of equity was also known as the court of conscience. Lord Browne-Wilkinson affirmed again that equity is conscience-driven when in *Westdeutsche v Islington London Borough Council [1996] AC 699*, he noted emphatically that *"Equity operates on the conscience of the owner of the legal interest. In the case of a trust, the conscience of the legal owner requires him to carry out the purposes for which the property was vested in him (express or implied) or which the law imposes on him by reason of his unconscionable conduct."*[5]

So the police while applying the law, are expected to act equitably. This is where the concept of enforcing the law simply for its own sake will lead to unfair and unconscionable

---

[5] Westdeutsche v Islington London Borough Council [1996] AC 699

decisions being made by officers. Built into this police discretion is Ethical behaviour and professional conduct. We shall examine this in a bit more detail later in the book.

The long and detailed historical examination of equity was necessary so that you can understand a major source of police ethical problems in the field. Police discretion is personal to each officer and there has to exist good basis to exercise it in order for that decision to be ethical. I therefore felt an historical analysis was needed to help you understand that Equity runs through the entire criminal justice system in all African societies.

Ethics and law differ in that ethics are social guidelines based on moral principles and values while laws are rules and regulations that have specific penalties and consequences when violated.

Ethics do not always have punishments (unless codified), fines or associated penalties when people fail to abide by them while laws do. This is why many people find

Ethics more challenging to practice compared with the Law.

So an officer has codified Ethics in rule and regulations and also have general Ethics that are result of personal maturity and knowledge as a police officer. Ethics are informed by Moral and Social standards; hence the more informed or trained you are, the better you will be at practicing Ethics as a police officer.

Ethical values and legal principles are usually closely related, but ethical obligations typically exceed legal duties. In some cases, the law mandates ethical conduct (where there is codification).

Generally speaking, ethics are often difficult to codify because of their sometimes subjective nature. So ethics can be a spectrum or scale of behaviour. The difference between legal and ethical issues stems from the division between the core areas of law and ethics; law controls what people can and cannot do, while ethics are moral standards that govern what people should or should not do.

Good ethics gives the law a good face. Good ethics can help fulfil the reasoning behind the law (the Spirit of it); rather than the letter of the law. (Many laws are not perfectly worded or targeted).

Ethics is the FOUNDATION of police discretionary powers in all countries as previously explained. (What you SHOULD DO based on the particular facts, within What the law says you MUST DO).

FIVE SPECTRUMS OF ETHICS IN POLICING

PRIVATE/PERSONAL ETHICS – This relates with how you conduct yourself privately as a police officer.

PROFESSIONAL ETHICS- Relates with how you conduct yourself in Public while on duty.

OPERATIONAL ETHICS – Relates to how you deal with suspects, evidence and Investigations. These are mostly away from the glare of the public.

INSTITUTIONAL ETHICS – Relates to your behaviour towards colleagues and the police organisation (Institution) you work for.

INHERENT ETHICS – Relates to your attitude towards the Rule of Law and your national Constitutional provisions in general.

A major misconception is that an officer who possesses private ethics will necessarily possess ethics in all areas noted above. This is not necessarily true. There are people who hold on to certain ethical belief based on their personal religious belief for instance; who will readily collect bribe at work. They see the two arenas as separate and distinct enough to warrant different responses.

It is possible to be Ethical in one lane and not in another. You can have private ethics but lack Professional Ethics. It is therefore important for officers to be trained in professional ethics as a mandatory professional competency factor.

CHAPTER TWO

WHY DOES ETHICS MATTER?

The essential question is: Why does ethics matter? In these days of the "end justifying the means" mentality in many circles, why does procedural and operational ethics matter in policing?

Someone once said that if you do not stand for something, then you will fall for anything. Moral ambiguity can prove to be the first stop on the path to a pattern of unethical and illegal behaviour by otherwise well-meaning officers across Africa.

Virtually everything done by a police officer has an ethical component. Either frontline dealing with the public or backup functions like analysts. Ethics is the one thing that is present in all police actions. From investigation techniques, to arrest, questioning and prosecution of offenders, the police is saddled with ethical duties based on the law and equity.

Across the continent, many law enforcement officers work on the slippery slope of situational ethics. The basis of situational ethics, a doctrine developed in the 1960s, is that there are no absolutes and there are times when it's appropriate to bend or even ignore certain moral principles if doing so serves a greater good.[6]

The practice of "situational ethics" can lead to a world where you don't have to obey the rules if you can convince yourself and articulate to your supervisors (in a law enforcement context) that your action is justifiable given the "totality of the circumstances."[7]

---

[6] https://www.policeone.com/police-jobs-and-careers/articles/3804919-Situational-ethics-and-the-moral-chaos-of-modern-policing/ accessed on 20 May 2017
[7] ibid

This natural moral ambiguity can lead to wildly varied responses to a given set of circumstances and opens the door to law enforcement critics who can readily find justification for their criticisms of police ethics.

It may also prove to be the first stop on the path to a pattern of illegal conduct by the rank and file officers. This is why ethical training has to be continuous and unrelenting.

So why does Ethics matter in policing? There are plenty of reason, and here are just a few of them:

- ➢ Officers are held to higher ethical standards by their community and the courts. This is only fair, given the enormous powers statutes and other legal instruments have given to the police over their fellow citizen.

- ➢ The news media is often watching closely. So any wrong misstep will become global news. Every officer is therefore an ambassador of the noble profession.

> Police officer's actions set an example (good or bad) for other officers and for the community. So how these are conducted matters.

> To protect your job and your career. Respect for the police will increase as officers become exemplars in ethical behaviour.

> It is actually easier to do your job as a police officer when others trust you. Ethics breed trust.

> Shame over ethical scandals can be unbearable for many officers; especially the innocent officers.

> Public trust is vital to good law enforcement. The more support officers get, the better the police will be at resolving most cases.

➢ You don't want to shame or embarrass your friends and family and ruin your reputation and police career as a result of avoidable scandal and misconduct.

ETHICAL BREACHES BY POLICE OFFICERS

In all police organisations, ethical breaches are usually either PEER INDUCED or PEER SUSTAINED.

It's either you saw colleagues do it and you copy the bad behaviour or you did it on your own but nobody called you to order or corrected you. This perpetuates the cycle of ethical violations by police officers.

Peer Induced ethical breach is the case of bad company corrupting good manners. A good officer is subjected to several ethical misbehaviours by peers and superiors over a period of time. The good officer will soon start to copy what he sees others do. This happens a lot especially to newly qualified officers.

Peer sustained ethical breach is the case of a badly behaving police office being allowed to get away with it without any correction from superior or any consequences for the bad behaviour. The officer will soon be entrenched in bad habits and behaviour that creates bad professional conduct.

Due to the colonial origin of policing in most African countries, there is a long standing mistrust between the police and the people they serve. With bad and corrupt government using the police to supress and harass the citizenry; the police have come to be seen as an extension of bad and unpopular governments across Africa.

The lack of effective ethical conducts consistently by police officers across the continent, has led to a crisis of confidence in the impartiality and fairness of the police.

SUBSTANTIVE v PROCEDURAL JUSTICE

What is the difference you may ask? The procedural law determines how a proceeding concerning the enforcement of substantive law will occur. Substantive law defines how the facts in the case will be handled, as well as how the crime is to be charged.

The common concern is that some police officers will break procedural law in order to enforce substantive law; done in the name of getting the job done. This is bad ethics. Procedural Law are there to ensure successful prosecution of suspects.

The constitutional landscape across Africa is different from country to country. But there are certain universal duties of the police that is well understood. Some of these are:

- ➢ Serving the Community
- ➢ Safeguarding Lives and Property
- ➢ Protecting the Innocent
- ➢ Keeping the Peace
- ➢ Ensuring the Rights of All to Liberty, Equality, and Justice

POLICE STANDARD OF BEHAVIOUR
Police officers should be responsible for their

own professional conduct. The necessity for professional growth is prevalent in all professions, especially in policing.

Officers should seek opportunities for expanded learning and continuous development of relevant skills and concepts.

Making ethical decisions within the Police is an absolute necessity in order to gain the confidence of the public that police officers serve. Ethical decision making does not mean making a decision that everyone agrees with.

It also does not mean making the same decision as what other officers would have made. It means making an ethical decision between competing choices.

ETHICS AND POLICING – A BRIEF HISTORY

Globally, policing has encountered many watershed moments brought on by various crisis and pressures in national police organisations. These moments in history have led to the operational ethics of the police being questioned, analysed and discussed. This book will cease to be a concise book, if it delves into these historical events in detail. More so, these events were mainly in the Western democracies, so cannot be fully compared with policing in Africa which is the focus of this book.

But a brief summary of the salient schools of thought may be helpful to the reader to give a comprehensive view of the turbulent evolution of thoughts and practices in police operational standards internationally.

1) At a time when there was crisis of political interference in policing in the United States, O. W Wilson was a chief of police who tried to create a new agenda for the professionalization of policing. Elliston and Feldberg (1985) described Wilson as a *'Moral administrator"* because his vison was of a highly technical and highly trained group of police officers operating to clear rules and independent of local politics, while acting with integrity and

impartiality. Many will say Wilson's vision is still relevant till today.

2) At another crisis point in the United States, during the pressures of the Vietnam war, William Westley (1970) and Jerome Skolnick (1975), debated whether the professional agenda set by Wilson could be met by any police organisation. For Westley, who was a specialist in police violence; the hostility between police and the public as well as the culture of isolation by the police will make the attainment of Wilson's vision impossible. He argued that a more open and accountable police organisation culture was needed to make any ethical vision attainable.

However, Skolnick believed that the inherent tension within the role of the police in society is in itself a problem. He felt that upholding the law while maintaining order were potentially difficult to reconcile. He questioned how an officer could reconcile the need to maintain order through cohesive force with the need to uphold individual rights and respect for the law. Skolnick's solution was that upholding the law had to come first.

3) The case of *Miranda v Arizona* was a major case in the US Supreme court whose verdict was seen as limiting police discretion. This was another crisis point. A decade on from this verdict, Herman Goldstein and W.K Muir (1977) contributed to the policing literature on good governance. Goldstein posited that the solutions was better management of the police.

   This requires better senior management team in the police organisation. These managers he stated; should be encouraged to formalise the informal and ensure rank and file officers were trained in the effective and proper use of operational discretion.

Muir on the other hand started his analysis from the other end of the spectrum through his observation of officers on the street. He concluded that morality is a product of individual officer's view of human nature. He asserted that while managers and trainers can influence behaviour and conduct of officers, individual officers have the free will to exercise choice about their style of policing and attitude towards the public.

Contrastingly, while Skolnick believed that the structural and social conditions of policing predetermines the morality of officers; Muir and Goldstein believed the free will and moral choices of individual officers is the dominant factor.

4) Another crisis point was the scandal surrounding the use of covert policing methods in the United States. There was a major outcry about the police use of deceptive policing methods and its

impact on privacy of citizens. Feldberg and Elliston argued that analyzing covert operations through the standard approach to moral philosophy like the utilitarian theory was flawed. They argued that a more complex understanding is needed which encompasses law and sociology in a joined up approach.

Gary Marx (1988) advanced this thinking in his discuss of the emerging surveillance society which he felt damaged privacy, trust and freedom of citizens. He canvassed a difference between *'ethical deception'* and *'deceptive ethics'*. According to Marx, ethical deception is a form of policing deception that is authorised by the citizenry as legitimate law enforcement tool and controlled by law. On the other hand, 'deceptive ethics' is the state doing by stealth what it could not do lawfully. He concluded that the difference between the two is not just a product of outcomes alone, but also of the collateral impacts on both the citizens and the reputation and perception of the police.

5) In the mid 1980s, another crisis rocked the police in America; that was perception of endemic widespread corruption. Against this background, Lawrence Sherman (1985) and Edwin Delattre (1989) stepped into this discussion. Delattre believed the solution was in "Character" of individual officers. He said the way to achieve ethical policing was to recruit and develop individuals who had the habit of integrity. This requires a stringent recruitment and vetting process of applicants with various tests implemented to reveal unethical predisposition.

But Sherman thought otherwise. He posited that the 'institutional environment' of temptation and impunity in which officers operates is more important a factor than the personal morality of individual officers. He believed that clamping down on small breach of ethics or corruption will avoid the need to deal with bigger infringements later on.

6) Finally, after the *"Rodney King"* beating race crisis in the United states, the issue of police brutality, covert policing and its use of force was revisited. In 1998, Joycelyn Pollock stirred by a decade-long debate about the role of the police and a renewed corruption scandal in many forces in the United States, canvassed a new theory of defining police as *"Public Servants"* instead of *"Crime Fighters"*. This emphasised the need of the police to build trust and reconciliation in communities.

It is no surprise that all the above authors and experts were Americans. The constitutional tradition in the USA has always viewed the police as agents of the executive with some suspicion. The police have always been one of the most powerful agent of the state power in every country; this is even more of the case in post colonial Africa.

There were similar trends and tension in the evolution of policing in Europe, Canada and Australia. They shared common theme of transition, crisis and search for renewal.

The foregoing brief summary has identified a number of common issues confronting the policing globally and of course in Africa. It has become a "vicious cycles" over the past century of policing.

In conclusion; the four main trends are:

> Crime Fighting. This is where the police are focused on a war on crime and criminality as a salient focus.

> This tended to be followed by a crisis of Corruption and other Scandals.

> There is then a reaction by society and state institutions which usually involve tightening of rules and procedures as well as reorganization of the police

institution itself.

➢ The last state of the cycle tends to be a commitment by the police to the new rules and norms. But this often is followed sooner or later by a drift back to crime fighting and the cycle repeats itself.

It is my hope that the foregoing brief summary has given you a global perspective of the challenge of ethics in policing. This is not just an African problem. It is a human problem. Anytime you give a human being power over others, the possibility of abuse is inevitable. That is why strong accountability systems are necessary to deter impunity and a relapse to bad practices.

That is why constant ethical training is needed to keep reminding officers of the emerging laws and societal expectation of them in their various African jurisdictions. It is my hope that this book will help you perform better your duties in an ever more challenging environment.

CHAPTER THREE

HOW BAD IS THE PROBLEM OF ETHICS?

Sir Robert Peel (the father of British policing) in 1829, set out a vision of a police constable patrolling on behalf and with the full support of his community. This connection between the police and the public is captured in the phrase *'the police are the public and the public are the police'.*

Peel's principles focus heavily on the importance of public support and emphasised the need for the police to secure and maintain public respect in all its action. This was known as the principle of "policing by consent."

In a functioning democracy, effective policing is usually by consent of the citizens. This is based on the pragmatic response that you can never have enough police officers in the field to be effective if a good proportion of any national population decides to break the law.

The concept of policing by consent creates an acknowledgement by the citizenry that they support the police and its work and therefore will be law abiding, by and large. This gives the police the time and resources to focus on the few that decides to break the law; given the compliance of a majority of the population.

The police need to count on the goodwill and cooperation of the public in carrying out their duties. Despite the challenges of their chequered colonial past and structures; the main difficulty to police organisations in many African countries in gaining the support of their citizens is the bad ethics and professional practices of many officers in national policing organisations across the continent.

The stories of police officers behaving badly is all too common on social media in many African countries.

The behaviour and conduct of officers in their public interactions is the single most important determinant of public perception of police in African countries. From extortions to brutality and abuses of all kinds, police in African countries do not have a good reputation with their citizenry, although the extent of negative ratings vary from country to country.

The most powerful factor to gaining legitimacy and buy-in from the people seems to be the ways in which police officers wield their authority. So if the police can get the ethics right; they can pretty much get everything else right over time.

Confidence in the police will also determine how much cooperation the police get from the people. Citizens are the eyes and ears of the police. Intelligence-led policing will be difficult without a cooperating population who are willing to supply information to the police.

I conducted a study into police operations in ten African countries made up of five Anglophone and five Francophone countries. I was interested in the main weaknesses of the police as perceived by the citizenry.

It was a surprise that the perceptions were pretty much the same in both Francophone and Anglophone countries.

KEY WEAKNESSES OF POLICE INSTITUTIONS IN AFRICA

1. **Misplaced Loyalty.** The loyalty tends to be on the fellow officers first, then to the government but not the people they serve.
2. **Cynicism.** Police view most citizens with suspicion. The population in turn view the police as corrupt, and dangerous.
3. **The Use of Force**. The police easily embrace force for all situations wherein a threat is perceived.
4. **"The Police as Victims" Mentality.** This concept is based on the idea that

the police are victims of public misunderstanding and scorn, of low wages and self-serving administrators.

5. **Preferential Application of the Law.** Decisions about whether to enforce the law, in any but the most serious cases, should be guided by what the law says and not who the suspect is.

6. **"The Police as Untouchables".** Police officers tend to find every means to impose punishment, including an arrest on fake charges.

7. **Rewards.** Police do very dangerous work for low wages, so it is proper to take any extra rewards the public wants to give them. One theory is that it is acceptable to accept any type of reward as long as it was given wholeheartedly by an individual to a police officer.

8. **Due Process.** It is only a means of protecting criminals at the expense of the law abiding and should be ignored whenever it is safe to do so.

9. **Corruption, Lying and Deception.** Many officers believe lying and

deception are an essential part of the police job, and even perjury should be used if it is necessary to protect yourself or get a conviction on a "bad guy".

In broad terms, individual unethical activities observed in police operations across Africa can be classified into the following key groups.

BRUTALITY
Individual police brutality is often a product of immaturity. It is caused partly by fear. Institutionalized brutality is a by-product of:

- ➢ Poor training.
- ➢ Peer support.
- ➢ Lax / incompetent supervision.

ABUSE OF AUTHORITY
This can be in the following forms:

- ➢ Legal abuse
- ➢ Physical abuse
- ➢ Verbal abuse

LYING
This can be in the form of:

- ➢ Falsifying Reports – Leads to credibility problem
- ➢ Falsifying Evidence – Can make the Guilty go free
- ➢ Cover-ups – Can affect more than the case at hand.
- ➢ Lying in Court – Contempt of court

SEXUAL MISCONDUCT
This manifests as any of the following:
- ➢ Sexual Bribery/extortion.
- ➢ Sexual liaisons with suspects.
- ➢ Voyeurism. – In or out of Custody
- ➢ Exposing the nakedness of suspects – Especially of opposite gender.

CRIMES FOR PROFIT
This breaches can occur as:
- ➢ Theft of Property or Exhibits
- ➢ Bribery – Giving and Accepting
- ➢ Extortion

DELIBERATE INEFFICIENCY
This is very visible when officers engage in:
- ➢ Sleeping on Duty
- ➢ Shirking Duty

PERSONAL ETHICAL EXERCISE-1

There is a debate in ethics over whether there can ever be situations in which it is morally justified to **intentionally violate an accepted ethical principle**.

- ➤ What do you think?
- ➤ Can there ever be specific situations in law enforcement in which
    - ✓ **it is morally permissible to lie?**
    - ✓ To **violate someone's rights?**
    - ✓ To **exploit or harm someone for the good of others**?
- ➤ Can you give examples?

_____

_____

_____

_____

_____

_____

_____

CHAPTER FOUR

ETHICAL CATEGORISATION OF POLICE OFFICERS

When officers act unethically, it's almost never because they don't know what the right thing to do is. They know; they just don't want to do it.

In a very real sense, ethics is less about "doing the right thing" than it is about "being the right kind of person."

Our ethical behaviour is based almost entirely on what kind of ethical character we have developed and how morally mature we are.

Edwin Delattre has been a leading figure on the subject of ethics in law enforcement for a long time, as well as an instructor at the FBI academy. In his book, *Character & Cops*, Delattre identifies four categories of police character. I will like us to briefly examine these categories.

THE BAD CHARACTER

Officers at this lowest level exemplify total, absolute and shameless self-interest. They seek opportunities to profit personally by victimizing others. They seem to think that others exist only to be exploited for their own personal advantage.

They are shameless in abusing their authority.

They are shrewd and without conscience; dangerous to life and property. Delattre refers to this group as *"meat-eaters,"* and maintains that they cannot be changed or "cured;" only identified and weeded out of the force.

THE WEAK CHARACTER

This group can be described as *"grasseaters."* These officers may not have harmful intentions, but are weak-willed and vulnerable to childish temptations and impulses. They exhibit a marked moral immaturity.

These officers cannot trust themselves in situations of temptation or pressure, because they lack self-control and self-discipline. They may be teachable (in contrast to the Bad Character folks), but they don't belong in positions of public trust if they do not change.

THE SELF-CONTROLLED CHARACTER

These officers possess greater self-discipline than the uncontrolled character, but they still tend to resent the higher ethical standards to which they are held as law enforcement officers. They may envy others who profit off of illegalities, but hold themselves back from participation through self-control.

Over time, these officers may feel a persistent tension between their inner desires and their professional duties.

While they may never commit crimes themselves, they often become unhappy, bitter, stressed, and burned out from the inner conflicts.

THE EXCELLENT CHARACTER

These officers have acquired and integrated habits of trustworthiness and honesty. These virtues have become second nature to them.

They are able to enjoy true peace of mind, because they know who they are and what they stand for. They live lives of integrity, becoming one good person, through and through.

They are incorruptible because they understand that money and power are not ends in themselves, but merely useful tools. Delattre maintains that only this group is worthy to bear the trust of public service in law enforcement.

Humans are notoriously inconsistent. Most of us have our moments of ethical greatness and others that we're not so proud of. But which of these categories do you think describes you most of the time? What kind of character do you see yourself having?

If your previous answer was anything less than the "Excellent Character," what steps could you take now to begin improving that and moving toward a higher level of ethical character?

STAGES AND PROGRESSION OF POLICE ATTITUDES FORMATION DURING THEIR CAREER[8]

Most new police officer come into the profession to do the right thing. They may have ideas of what impact they wish to make in their communities. But over time, circumstances lead to totally different officer emerging from the strain of the institutional culture of the police organisation they belong.

So what are the stages of the evolution of a typical officer from innocent embrace of the rules to possible complete disdain for the same rules. There are a few. But with

---

[8] This attitude scale was originally developed by Donald Osgood to describe stages people go through in any organization.

continuous training, an officer can turn the circle and become ethical and committed. But to get to that end position, the officer would have gone through the following stages in attitudinal development.

IDEALISTIC STAGE

This stage is exemplified by new officers, confident of their values and ability to succeed. High expectations and goals, but confidence is naïve and idealistic. This tend to be a textbook understanding of what being a police officer is.

FRUSTRATED STAGE

Idealism crashes into wall of reality. Present circumstances are a far cry from original goals and desires. Initial reactions are often dominated by fear, indecision, and anxiety. The world is not

so simple as we had believed or hoped. Young officers at this stage might be susceptible to negative peer pressure.[9]

---

[9] Some of the stage comments were adapted from Ethics Applied, Edition 3.0 (Pearson Educational Publishing, 2000.)

DEFIANT STAGE

Fear and indecision are overcome as we realise that we have to take some responsibility in our own hands. However, actions taken at this stage are usually negative and destructive, especially when covert or hidden.

Some people continue to live for years with this hidden, internal resentment before they lash out in defiant rage. This can pollute relationships with family, colleagues, supervisors, and even society at large.

RESIGNED STAGE

Some people who have harboured covert defiance eventually slip into resignation to the disappointment and aimlessness of their lives. The lights go out in their eyes. They may continue punching the clock to get to retirement, but they have lost all joy in their lives and their jobs. This stage and the defiant one are when officers are most vulnerable to making poor decisions that could cost them their jobs and careers.

AWARE STAGE

Hopefully, some self-analysis goes on and an officer eventually become aware of some of the damage that his defiance and resignation have caused to his own life and other people he cares about. This awareness is the first step toward developing a more positive outlook on life. The officer has now realised that he must change.

DECISIVE STAGE

The officer consciously does something different and positive, taking responsibility for his own life and happiness. These changes begin the process of making his life more vital, creative, and meaningful.

COMMITMENT STAGE

This is the final result of the positive life changes an officer makes. He does not expect perfection of himself or others, yet he is committed to attempt his best ideals, with his best abilities, while remaining realistic about his talents and results.

This is not a fragile idealism like before, but a purposeful and prudent devotion (sincere, flexible, and open to learn and grow further).

These stages demonstrate how easy it is to lose a good officer from the defiant stage of the attitude formation. This is why police organisations across Africa have to invest heavily in continuous professional development of the rank and file officers. It is only through consistent high quality training that the trajectory of an officer's attitude formation can be rescued from bad to committed.

REFELCTION EXERCISES

Can you recall all of the stages that you can remember going through during your career.

In which stage or stages do you see yourself now?

What steps could you take now that might help you move on toward more positive attitudes that would allow you to enjoy your job and your life more?

What can caring officers do to help a fellow officer who is exhibiting these negative attitudes, but is not yet aware of their presence and destructive potential?

CHAPTER FIVE

THE PATHOLOGY OF POLICE ETHICS

Ethical breaches by police officers are products of various causal factors. Some are individual to each officer, but by vast the majority has to do with the institutional sub-culture and poor accountability system in the organisations.

The salient causes of ethical misadventures in police officers are as follows:

TRAINED INCAPACITY

Trained incapacity refers to that state of affairs in which one's abilities function as blind spots. Training a person to do a job one way simultaneously trains that person to not do the job any other way. Training for one set of conditions becomes dysfunctional when conditions change.

OCCUPATIONAL PSYCHOSIS

Occupational psychosis is a product of the socialization process. The new member must replace values and beliefs with those of the subculture. In policing this is known as the "John Wayne" Syndrome. This syndrome can best be understood as:

"A state of mind of new recruits which the individual perceives that they are the roughest, toughest, badass that walked the streets. Though in reality, they are just lonely people that have low self-esteems. Because without the gun they are nothing, nor have anything else to offer to society. In other words, they're just a pussy with a gun."[10]

---

[10] adapted from a similar definition from
http://www.urbandictionary.com/define.php?term=John%20Wayne%20S
yndrome

Symptoms of this psychosis include, Dualism-viewing the world as good vs. bad, "You are either for or against me." Loss of sense of humour, distancing from outsiders and preoccupation with perceived organizational value system.

FUNDAMENTAL AMBIVALENCE
A form of occupational blindness or tunnel vision. A way of seeing becomes a way of not seeing anything different. Every event is screened through the value laden viewpoint of the predetermined subculture.

SACREDIFICATION
Sacredification is the process wherein bureaucratic norms become sacred values. Police officers develop an over-reliance on organisational symbols and provide these symbols a legitimacy of their own. Organisational fear is a by-product of the sanctification process. The values become so accepted no one dares challenge the system.

GOAL DISPLACEMENT

Adherence to rules, originally devised as means, becomes transformed into ends. Ends become obscure or lost. Means become sacred. People or organization lose sight of their mission.

ESPIRIT D'CORPS

Group cohesiveness, necessary for successful military operations, has a destructive component for civilian agencies. It is the belief that the "worst" of us is better than the "best" of them. We have "bad cops" because "good cops" protect them.

ORGANISATIONAL ARROGANCE

This is caused by a perceived power differential. The organization is powerful; therefore, the member is also powerful. The citizen, representing no one, is not powerful and not worthy of respect. The result is institutionally sanctioned rudeness.

The causes examined above, exert pressure and influence on police officers to behave in a certain way. This is exacerbated by the collective crowd influence of group behaviour. Many officers tend to play along to fit into the group.

A fundamental skill required by a police officer is being self aware. An officer need to know himself so well, he can recognise when he begins to act out of character. He then reign in his own excesses through self censure and discipline of training.

EXPERIENCE v PROCEDURE

Many officers rely more heavily on experience than department procedure. Personal experience is inherently flawed; it rests on subjective impressions filtered through biased expectations. Officers often remember when a technique to a problem works, but forget the many times in which a similar approach did not work.

An over reliance on experience tend to breed bad ethics. Procedures are objective standards and should be followed. Official procedures tend to have built-in checks and balances meant to protect you. So following these official steps enhances your ethical posture and capabilities.

CHAPTER SIX

POLICE ETHICS AND ACCOUNTABILITY

"Police forces like to claim that each high-profile abuse is an aberration, committed by a `rogue' officer. But these human rights violations persist because the accountability systems are so defective."[11]

The greater the officer's ability to avoid accountability, the greater the amount of police misconduct. The police subculture often defeats accountability. We have bad cops because good cops protect them.

---

[11] Kenneth Roth executive director of the human rights watch.

The police need to know who they work for – the people. The authority that they have belongs to the people. Across Africa, people are demanding more accountability from the police. They are demanding more ethical conduct and practices as well as procedures.

Law enforcement institutions are entrusted with a diverse set of tasks requiring a high degree of integrity within police agencies and their oversight. Where this does not function well, law enforcement officers may become vulnerable to acting unlawfully and outside their remit.

In post-conflict societies in particular, but also in many non-conflict situations, police reform interventions are much needed, often in the form of retraining for police officers with a particular focus on human rights principles. In addition, a longer-term effort is required to establish a framework for police oversight and accountability in order to strengthen integrity within systems of policing.[12]

Apart from their own national constitutional provisions, African countries have signed up to most if not all of the relevant international treaties and protocols as adopted by the African Union. So there are so many accountability tools in existence to ensure the police do act within the law and the provisions of equity.

The African public expects high ethical standards from their police. Trust in the police is vital – from top officers, to the most junior police officers. Police ethics (their honesty, their integrity, their impartiality, their openness) should be beyond reproach.

---

[12] William G. O'Neill, *Police Reform and Human Rights*: A HURIST Document (New York, Joint Human Rights Strengthening Programme of the United Nations Development Programme and the Office of the High Commissioner for Human Rights (HURIST), 2004). In the past decade, a number of publications have been released collating the main lessons learned in relation to police reform in post-conflict situations but also as a component of conflict prevention strategies. See for example David H. Bayley, *Democratizing the Police Abroad:* What to Do and How to Do It, Issues in International Crime (Washington, D.C., United States of America, Department of Justice, National Institute of Justice, June 2001)

Above all, this requires effective accountability and leadership to create a culture where high standards of behaviour are the norm. High standards (of both conduct and accountability) also need to be demonstrated by those charged by national legislations with holding the police to account.

The police accountability structures and systems vary from one African country to another. Some of strict structures of accountability (like in South Africa); while others have lose array of agencies saddled with this function but are largely ineffective (as is the case in Nigeria).

A small number of countries have robust independent complaints structure in place; while others do not have any independent oversight of the operations of the police.

There is need for statutory police oversight protocols that is independent in most of the countries in Africa. These protocols should also enshrine into law, the operational independence of the police.

To be certain that a high level of accountability is built into any police oversight structure; certain values must be paramount to policy makers. So there needs to be a strong and continuing focus on:

> ➢ clarity of responsibility and accountability;
> ➢ developing a sustainable culture of embedding high ethical standards; and
> ➢ robust effective ethical leadership.

Effective accountability requires an effective and independent complaint system which does not exist in most African countries. This is partly due to the politicisation of the police by politicians across the continent.

The police have become a branch of the ruling party in many countries, so much so that a criticism of the police is taken as an attack of the ruling party. This scenario does not promote effective accountability by the police to the public.

According to the United Nations,[13] effective police accountability involves many different actors representing the different layers of modern-day democracies. This will include government representatives, the parliament, the judiciary, civil society actors and independent oversight bodies such as national human rights institutions. Primarily, it involves the police themselves.[14]

Key elements of an effective police accountability system include:[15]

> ➢ Legislation (in line with international human rights law) specifying the functions and powers of the police.
> ➢ Practical instructions based on the legislation that reflect both the spirit and the letter of the law.
> ➢ Opportunities for the public to voice their concerns.

---

[13] United Nations Handbook on police accountability, oversight and integrity, 2011. Sales No. E.11.IV.5
[14] ibid
[15] ibid

➢ Policies that set priorities on how to deploy police capacity.

➢ Adequate police training, both basic and ongoing.

➢ Equipment that is adequate for prescribed police functions.

➢ Proper reporting procedures and facilities.

➢ Adequate supervision that supports officers in carrying out their duties professionally and reporting these correctly.

➢ A working culture that promotes transparency and evaluation.

➢ Monitoring of police actions and operations by both police leadership and external organs.

➢ Complaints procedures, both for making complaints to the police directly and to independent bodies.

➢ Fair and effective procedures and policies on how to deal with misconduct, including both disciplinary and criminal codes, adequate investigative capacity, procedures for punishment and appeal procedures

➢ An independent body to oversee such procedures.
➢ Scrutiny and oversight involving feedback to the police in order to improve future activities and prevent future wrongdoings.
➢ Evaluation and complaints procedures that contribute to the development of new policies, procedures and instructions.
➢ Reliable statistics on police performance, related both to effectiveness in dealing with crime and public order, as well as to their integrity and public confidence.
➢ Procedures for overseeing the feedback, evaluation and complaints procedures and statistics

According to the United Nations, efforts to enhance police oversight and accountability must focus on three key, related priorities.

Firstly, where policing has been militarised[16] and may be undemocratic and authoritarian, efforts must be made to enhance civilian control over the police.

Secondly, it is necessary to increase public confidence in the police by upgrading levels of police service delivery as well as by investigating and acting in cases of police misconduct.[17]

Finally, reducing corruption within the police is crucial. Corruption and bad ethics go together. All corrupt officers are automatically unethical in their behaviour.

The key players in enhancing police accountability are police officers themselves, as the prime bearers of responsibility for the integrity of the police force. The next most important players are independent police oversight bodies. Other State institutions, most notably the Ministry in charge of the

---

[16] That is, military in style, culture and operations and sometimes in fact, when the police have been part of the military.
[17] ibid

police and civil society, are also of crucial importance.

The mechanisms established by States to protect people's rights, establish and maintain order and guarantee stability and security are usually referred to collectively as the security sector.[18]

An important actor in the security sector is the police, whose functions, as a minimum, are:

➢ Prevention and detection of crime

➢ Maintenance of public order

➢ Provision of assistance to the public

---

[18] It is generally agreed that the security sector includes "core security actors (e.g. armed forces, police, gendarmerie, border guards, customs and immigration, and intelligence and security services); security management and oversight bodies (e.g. ministries of defence and internal affairs, financial management bodies and public complaints commissions); justice and law enforcement institutions (e.g. the judiciary, prisons, prosecution services, traditional justice systems); and non-statutory security forces (e.g. private security companies, guerrilla armies and private militia)."

In order to carry out these functions, the police have certain powers, namely the power to arrest and detain and the power to use force.

It is precisely this monopoly on the use of force[19] and the power to arrest and detain that place the police in a unique and sensitive position within the democratic State, so that adequate control mechanisms are required to ensure that these powers are consistently used in the public interest.[20] Like any other public service, the police must operate with impartiality at all times.

This is not a book on police accountability. But it is important to state that effective accountability is a powerful deterrence to bad

---

[19] In most countries, the police are the only State body that may legally use force to maintain order (in times of peace). Others are allowed to use force only in self-defence. This is referred to as a police monopoly on the use of force in times of peace.

[20] The notion that the State and all its institutions are to serve the public interest is reflected in article 1 of the International Code of Conduct for Public Officials (General Assembly resolution 51/59, annex) which states: "A public office, as defined by national law, is a position of trust, implying a duty to act in the public interest. Therefore, the ultimate loyalty of public officials shall be to the public interests of their country as expressed through the democratic institutions of government." The International Code of Conduct for Public Officials is recommended to Member States "as a tool to guide their efforts against corruption".

ethical practices in the police. A more accountable police organisation tends to be more ethical than an unaccountable one.

Therefore, the police leadership must be granted sufficient autonomy to decide, within an established budgetary framework and in line with laws and policies, how to respond to law-and-order situations and how to allocate resources, based on their professional expertise and intelligence as well as on their community contacts, subsequently accounting for their decisions. This is known as operational independence.[21]

The operational independence of the police leadership filters down to rank-and-file officers, where it takes the form of discretion (or discretionary powers). While on duty, a police officer typically has discretionary power in deciding which deviant behaviour to act on (obviously, acting within the bounds established in national law and policy). Exercising some discretion is at the very heart

---

[21] ibid

of policing: not every offence is worthy of police action nor is police action always the best solution to a problem.[22]

Additionally, as previously noted in Chapter one, police officers typically have some room for manoeuvre when using police powers, with the authority to make decisions on such matters as how much force to use and on whether to carry out arrests or searches.

Operational independence requires police:[23]

> ➤ To have a high degree of professionalism and independence from political influences.
> ➤ To act in conformity with the law and established policies.

---

[22] For a more elaborate discussion of operational independence see Anneke Osse, Understanding Policing: A Resource for Human Rights Activists (Amsterdam, Amnesty International Nederland, 2006), chapter 4.

[23] This is why the Patten Commission, responsible for formulating reforms for the police in Northern Ireland in the late 1990s, suggested the use of the term "operational responsibility" rather than "operational independence" so as to emphasize that the police must never escape scrutiny (A New Beginning: Policing in Northern Ireland—The Report of the Independent Commission on Policing for Northern Ireland, 1999, available from www.nio.gov.uk/a_new_ beginning_in_policing_in_northern_ireland.pdf. Accessed 23 December 2009.

➤ To operate on the basis of public consent (within the framework of the law), as evidenced by levels of public confidence.

➤ To take responsibility for their decisions and operations, accepting liability when required, and to exhibit full transparency in decisions and openness to external scrutiny

In other words, good policing is policing that is both effective and fair. Police who are ineffective, or illegitimate or unfair, in protecting the public against crime will lose the public's confidence.[24] Good policing is policing with legitimacy on the basis of public consent, rather than repression. Murphy and others later declared that:

"A legitimate institution's entitlement to have its rules and decisions obeyed is conferred by the public, and does not rest on the

---

[24] Kristina Murphy, Lyn Hinds and Jenny Fleming, "Encouraging public cooperation and support for police", Policing and Society, vol. 18, No. 2 (June 2008), pp. 136-155; United States, Department of Justice, Office of Community Oriented Policing Services and International Association of Chiefs of Police, Building Trust Between the Police and the Citizens They Serve: An Internal Affairs Promising Practices Guide for Local Law Enforcement (2009).

institution's power to impose its rules/directions."[25]

An ethical police organisation will readily earn the trust of the public to be able to function with public consent. Police accountability is essential to instil ethical behaviour and practices in the police.

Looking across Africa, most States do not have an accountable and operationally independent police service. It is hoped that the direction of travel will change to make this a thing of the past as Africa looks ahead to a brighter and awesome future.

---

[25] ibid

CHAPTER SEVEN

WHAT SHAPES THE MINDS OF POLICE OFFICERS

It could be said that police work touches more lives than any other profession, whether directly or indirectly in all African States. Certainly, it remains as the cornerstone of virtually all government functions.

Yet police organisations are also one of the most misunderstood agency of government all over Africa.

People naturally project their satisfaction or otherwise of the government in power on the police. So a good government will tend to give people the impression the police is also good; while a bad government will give the police organisation a very bad image as well.

While many of the negative perception of police institutions are as a result of the governmental system within which they function; there are many self-inflicted wounds on the police caused by the police themselves through many unethical and illegal activities witnessed daily by citizens all over Africa.

So what shapes the minds of police officers. Since nobody is born a police officer, the paradigms and worldview of police officers are shaped by factors in their environment. If we can determine which factors have positive and which ones have negative impacts; then we can determine what to avoid.

We are shaped by what we are exposed to. This can be Information, mode of behaviour modelled by others and even cultural values we hold in esteem.

OBJECTIVE v SUBJECTIVE INFORMATION

There are two main sources of Information available to police officers. The subjective information sources and skewed sources that reflects only a prejudicial or personal view that may not agree with the norm.

The objective sources are pretty much mainstream views that reflects society norm and more likely to be fair compared to the subjective sources.

Subjective information is based on personal opinions, interpretations, points of view, emotions and judgment. It is considered ill-suited for decision making in policing. An objective perspective is one that is not influenced by emotions, opinions, or personal feelings - it is a perspective based in fact, in things quantifiable and measurable.

While subjective information is personal opinions, assumptions, interpretations and beliefs; objective information is based on observation of measurable facts. Newspaper editorials, blogs, and comments on the Internet are examples of subjective sources of information.

Encyclopaedias, textbooks, reputable news reporting are examples of objective information sources. As a police officer, subjective sources are poor and inadequate information sources and your decision should not be based on what is glimpsed from these subjective sources.

Objective sources are fairer and more defensible. They are analysis or facts based compared to subjective sources. This book also is an example of an objective source of information.

The more objective information you have at your disposal, the better will be your subjective judgement in every situation. Even if you are applying a skewed standard in a situation; an abundance of pre existing objective information will strengthen your subjectivity. So police officers should engage in more objective sourcing of information to bolster their subjective narratives.

POLICE INFORMATION SOURCES.

What are the dominant information sources that shape the mentality of police officers? For many police officers in Africa, there is an overreliance on emotional sources:

- ➢ War stories
- ➢ Personal experiences
- ➢ Rumours.
- ➢ Fictional crime stories.
- ➢ Tales and myths by colleagues and superiors.
- ➢ Personal beliefs
- ➢ Organisational mythology.

Consequently, there is an under-reliance on factual sources:

- ➢ Established procedures
- ➢ Training
- ➢ Case law
- ➢ Research Reports
- ➢ Professional Journals
- ➢ Text books

POLICE SUB-CULTURE.

This alpha male subculture that many officers have tends to have a corrosive influence on the rank and file. This mind-set emphasises collective experience over training and procedure. It emphasises group loyalty over duty.

This kind of outlook is built on distrust of outsiders. This has led to many police organisations in Africa referring to the public they are meant to serve as *"Civilians"*. This creates a they and us mentality.

The colonial tradition of housing police officers in dedicated estates has also serve to separate the police from the public, thus reinforcing this subculture of distrust of outsiders.

The ultimate effect this sub culture is that it alters the definition of what success looks like to an officer. There invariably develops a divide between what the police organisation's view of success is and what officers think it is.

- ➢ **Police Department view of Success**
  - ➢ Community focus.
  - ➢ Problem addressed.
  - ➢ Appropriate approved procedure used.
  - ➢ Accurate record of event.
  - ➢ Actions taken legally/morally defensible.

- ➢ **Police Subculture view of Success**
  - ➢ Officer focus.
  - ➢ Problem masked.
  - ➢ Least demanding procedure used (shortcuts).
  - ➢ Self-serving record of event.
  - ➢ Actions often questionable, sometimes illegal.

SUPERVISION

Effective supervision is crucial if the mind of an officer is to be shaped correctly for the benefit of the organisation and the general public. Officers are susceptible to bad habits just like anybody else. They see things that puts them under stress and will see short cuts to cope with it. Peer and leadership supervision is essential.

Ultimately, people are responsible for their own behaviour. Each officer must make it clear to colleagues that improper behaviour will not be tolerated in his/her presence.

Each officer must intervene quickly to prevent/stop improper conduct from fellow officers. Peer counsellors should be trained and deployed across the police organisation. These are taught to help fellow officers express feelings of guilt, personal failure and fear.

Unfortunately, in many police organisations too many supervisors are more interested in being liked by officers than in holding them accountable for their behaviour. These leaders have forgotten that supervision in the police is not a popularity contest. Supervisors must make expectations clear and hold subordinates accountable for their behaviour.

Top level officers must clarify and solidify organisational expectations to all supervisors as well as the rank and file. Leadership must hold supervising officers accountable for the behaviour of their officers. People who will not/cannot supervise others must be removed from supervision.

Internal discipline is only as effective as the top level officers want it to be. The leadership must be fair, but abuses of authority and inappropriate conduct must be handled quickly and firmly.

A general consensus is that a police department has as much misbehaviour as it is willing to tolerate. This is due to the fact that police officers (due to the command and control structure) tend to pretty much obey orders of their superiors in most part. So a police leadership with zero tolerance to misconduct can pretty much stamp it out if it wants to.

CHAPTER EIGHT

POLICE ETHICAL DECISION-MAKING FRAMEWORK

As previously stated, ethical decision making is not intended to create a uniform singular outcome. Different officers can arrive at different outcomes over the same facts and they all could still have acted ethically.

It is a product of what each officer knows about the situation, their training and skill as well as their assessment of the facts.

But if properly trained and guided around certain universal principles, we can begin to see a commonality of response over the same facts.

In making ethical decisions, there has to be certain institutional principles and parameters set by the police organisation to guide its officers. These I call *policing principles*.

Additionally, individual officers must then apply their own test in every situation to ensure they are not only operating within these institutional principles but using their best judgement. This is what I call, the *standard of behaviour* befitting a police officer.

The *policing principles* reflect the Institutional attitudes and aspirations that in turn serve to guide the *standard of behaviour* and shape the policing culture in African countries.

The combination of principles and standards of behaviour should encourage consistency between what people believe in and aspire to, and what they do.

ESSENTIAL VALUES THAT SHAPES THE STANDARD OF BEHAVIOUR IN POLICING:
In making a determination as to the ethical status of a decision you are about to make, an

officer should consider these three basic factors at all times.

Legality – Does the decision in a particular situation have its basis in law. This is fundamentally critical as a police officer is also know as Law Enforcement Officer. So acting legally is a key expectation of police officers. But the knowledge of the officer comes into play here. An officer must have sufficient knowledge of the law to be able to recall it in operational situations. This is why training on a continuous basis is recommended, to allow officers to be abreast of new developments in statutes law and emerging legal precedents.

Necessity – Is the decision strictly necessary, given the circumstances of the respective situation. As there are many powers and tools available to officers to deal with situations in the field, you need to ask if what you are about to do is absolutely necessary in light of the circumstances.

Proportionality – is the decision in proportion to the seriousness of the offense and the legitimate objective to be achieved?

Are you over reacting? Must you effect an arrest or can you just give a verbal warning? Is your action proportional to the infringement? Will your response meet the legitimate demands of the law without leaving the citizens concerned distrusting of the police?

These three self-assessment values will help and guide an officer in making the right decision in every situation.

So when making a decision as a police officer, ask yourself these three questions:

> ➢ **Is this Legal.**
> ➢ **Is it Necessary**
> ➢ **Is it Proportionate.** (Am I over-reacting)

THE THREE OVERARCHING TEST GUIDE TO INDIVIDUAL ETHICAL DECISION MAKING

The foregoing values come out of some overarching value systems and behavioural tests. These are:

CRITICAL THINKING TEST

The Critical Thinking Test asks a series of "yes" or "no" questions to determine whether or not an officer should proceed with an action.

- ➢ Is my action legal?

- ➢ Will the end result be good?

- ➢ Will it work?

- ➢ Is there a better, less harmful way to achieve the same goal?

- ➢ Will my decision undermine or contradict another equally important principle?

- ➢ Even if the end result is good, do the means violate an ethical principle?

- ➢ Can my decision be justified if it is made public?

THE MEDIA TEST

A similar but simpler tool, the Media Test requires an officer to answer one simple question:

> ➤ "How would I feel if my decision made the front page tomorrow?"

This reminds officers that all too often, perception becomes reality and that it may not be enough just to be able to justify our actions if they cause the public to seriously question police practices and tactics.

The Media Test recognises that the public does not always see things the same way the law enforcement community does. It takes into consideration that, because police officers are ultimately public servants, they must be cognizant of what the public's perceptions are regarding police both on and off the job.

THE INTUITIVE TEST

Perhaps the simplest test of all is the gut/intuitive Test. The gut test essentially relies on instinct and the belief that, deep down, all officers can intuit the right decision.

Essentially, the Gut Test relies on the principle that if it feels wrong, it probably is wrong.

This is not to be confused with the difference between feeling good and bad, but between right and wrong. There are plenty of times that things that feel bad are right, and things that feel good are wrong.

THE MODEL ETHICAL POLICE ORGANISATION.

Institutionally, the police organisation should also promote certain values that will help to encourage and entrench ethical behaviour amongst its officers.

After a review of many police ethical and professional standards in Africa and the developed nations, I have concluded that the following fourteen values need to be promoted in one form or another by police organisations in Africa.

These are:
1. Fairness
2. Accountability

3. Honesty
4. Integrity
5. Impartiality
6. Leadership
7. Flexibility
8. Openness
9. Respect
10. Selflessness
11. Responsibility
12. Commitment to the Rule of Law
13. Professionalism
14. Love of Country

These philosophies should underpin and strengthen the existing ethical procedures in different African countries. Our research shows that African countries fall into three main categories when it comes to the existence of a robust ethical framework within their police organisations.

> ➤ Some have good ethical policy framework and are trying to operationalise it with some success.
> ➤ Some have policy framework but only on paper as there is no evidence of its operational impact.

> Others do not have any framework at all other than some verbal assurances and pontifications.

Now let us look at these values in some detail.

Fairness – This relates to the consistency and equity in officers' decisions and processes, in dealing with the community and each other

Accountability – An officer should remain accountable before the law and accept responsibility for his decisions and actions. An officer will guard against the abuse of the powers, which their office affords them and will oppose and draw attention to malpractice and wrongdoing by others.

Honesty – An officer will be honest and act with integrity at all times, and will not compromise or abuse his position. Officers are expected to be sincere and truthful.

Also needed is courage in doing what he/she believes to be right while ensuring that policing decisions are not influenced by improper considerations of personal gain.

Officers will not knowingly make false, misleading or inaccurate oral or written statements.

Integrity – The police will discharge their duties with honesty and will ensure that they do not place themselves under any financial or other obligation, which might influence the performance of their duties.

They will declare any private interests, which may conflict with their duties and take steps to avoid such conflict. Finally, integrity will require an officer to neither solicit nor accept the offer of any gift, gratuity or hospitality that could compromise your impartiality

Impartiality & Objectivity – Officers must act fairly and impartially, without prejudice and solely in terms of the public interest. They will discharge their duties with objectivity and without favour or malice.

Leadership – Officers should be approachable and consistent when dealing with colleagues, partners and the community. Strongly commit to the values of the organisation. Guide, trust, develop and empower colleagues to deliver for the team. Inspire participation and commitment through a shared vision.

Flexibility – Officers are open minded and adaptive to change. They should adopt an attitude of continuous improvement and encourage creativity. Build partnerships with the local communities. Officers are expected to welcome differences and practise tolerance.

Openness – This requires that an officer perform their duties in an open and transparent manner; submit their decisions and actions to appropriate scrutiny and will respond positively to criticism.

They will give reasons for their decisions and restrict information only when the wider public interest demands. They will be open and truthful about their actions while maintaining the confidentiality of information entrusted to them in accordance with the law.

Respect – based on human dignity, cultural awareness, respect for individual needs and differences. Accept diversity with tolerance and understanding. Listen with patience, value opinions and provide feedback when required. An officer working with respect is usually appreciative of and acknowledge the efforts of others.

Selflessness – Officers are expected to act in the public interest. They are supposed to focus on the public good and not their personal gain or benefit.

Responsibility – Police officers should accept personal responsibility for their own actions and omissions and act with resolve, tolerance and restraint in the discharge of their duties.

They will ensure that their actions are at all times lawful, reasonable and proportionate and take ownership of those actions and decisions made in the course of their duties. They will take responsibility for observance of these principles and promote them through leadership and personal example.

Commitment to the Rule of Law – An ethical police officer must be committed to the rule of law, regardless of its shortcomings.

Professionalism – A professional officer will show commitment and lead by example. Contributing to the professional knowledge pool of the organisation, officers will be accountable to both internal and external stakeholders. A professional officer will maintain high personal standards, taking pride in his appearance and conduct.

With service excellence as a goal, officers will communicate openly, honestly and consistently.

Love of Country – Above all, an ethical officer will have a heart for public service. They will have a love for their country and their people. This love for country will be an essential sustaining factor in hard situations.

CHALLENGING AND REPORTING ETHICAL BREACHES

A good police officer should feel confident to report, challenge or take action against the conduct of colleagues which has fallen below the standards of professional behaviour.

Officers must be encouraged never to ignore unethical or unprofessional behaviour by policing colleagues, irrespective of the person's rank, grade or role.

Rank and file should have a positive obligation to question the conduct of colleagues that falls below the expected standards and, if necessary, challenge, report or take action against such conduct.

If you feel you cannot question or challenge a colleague directly, you should report your concerns through a line manager, a force reporting mechanism or other appropriate channel.

WHISTLEBLOWER POLICY

The policing organisations across Africa should produce ethics code that will protect whistle-blowers according to the law of the land. This will be constructed slightly differently in individual nations. But the overall object will remain the same. That is encouraging ethical breaches to be reported confidentially and the witnesses protected by law from any form of harassment or witch-hunting.

ETHICAL CODE FOR EACH NATION

This will be the *Code of Ethics* for the principles and standards of professional behaviour for the policing profession in each of the member states of the Africa Union.

This code will need to be produced after consultation will national stakeholders but built on the overarching principles agreed at the continental level. To be effective, there will need to be national peculiarities to these codes to reflect the national nuanced requirements of each country.

The aim of this national policing Code of Ethics is to support each officer of the policing profession to deliver the highest professional standards in their service to the public.

The code must make clear the ethical principles that the police authorities expect to guide officers' decisions, whatever the context, and it must be clear about what happens if those expectations are not met. That is what a good code should aim to achieve.

In many African countries, policing has not, (sadly) yet adopted all the hallmarks of a profession. A good *Code of Ethics* will be one step towards obtaining full professional status for policing, similar to that seen in medicine and law for instance.

Once adopted, this code of ethics must be codified into statutes in all African nations. This will give it the force of law and take it away from any misunderstanding that it may be only advisory.

ETHICAL DECISION MODEL

There should be a primary decision-making model for police organisations with regards to possible breaches of ethical codes. This will allow for consistency of standards in dealing with breaches all over the country. In major incidents, the decision model can also aid decision making in the first place, not just the breach.

There are different types of models and there is no one size fits all. So a decision model will need to be produced that will reflect the peculiar landscape of jurisprudence and administrative structure of each nation.

The model places the Code of Ethics at the centre of all decision making. This reminds those in the policing profession that they should consider the principles and expected standards of behaviour set out in the Code at every stage of making decisions.

Breaches of the Code of Ethics will not always involve misconduct or require disciplinary proceedings. Breaches will range from relatively minor shortcomings in conduct, performance or attendance through to gross misconduct and corruption. Different procedures must be put in place according to the type of unprofessional behaviour or misconduct alleged.

It is not my intention in this book to produce a code for each African Union member states. That will only be possible through bespoke engagement with each country, reflecting its peculiarities. I however, hope this book has opened your eyes to see what is possible.

FINALLY
Ethics has become the backbone of all effective police operations in Africa. In fact, African countries have been coming together in the past few years to create continent-wide protocols and reports to assist with the creation of common standards in policing ethos.

I have reproduced some of these protocols as appendices in this book to give the reader an idea of the ambition of African nations in this area. Developing national esoteric police ethical standards and protocols will need to happen in all member states using the universal guiding principles already agreed at continental level.

Together with robust political will and implementation zeal; this continent will hopefully begin to develop effective 'policing by consent' framework that will build ethical polices organisations across the continent of Africa.

What does POLICE mean?

P – Professional

O – Organised – *Procedurally Sound*

L – Lawful

I – Intelligent – *Educated and trained.*

C – Community-oriented

E – Ethical

PERSONAL ETHICAL EXERCISE-2

An urgent request is put through to your station inviting you to an address where screams are heard. The caller is anonymous! On getting to the address you discover that nothing appears amiss. However, you insist on entering the address because you do not feel comfortable.

You look around and spot a number of bags on a table which you open and found full of cash. You therefore arrest the owner of the house and seize the bags.

What issues does this scenario raise in relation to Ethics?

ETHICAL EXERCISE 2 - ANALYSIS

Ethics & Professional Conduct Issues

> ➢ You insist on entering the house without a proper explanation to the owners. Why!

> ➢ Under what powers are the bags of cash seized?

> ➢ Is anything explained to the owners?

> ➢ Is a receipt for the seizure given to the owners?

> ➢ Is standard operational procedure being followed at all?

> ➢ Is there an evidence log?

> ➢ Is there a completed chain of custody form?

Does any of these questions raise issues with the professional conduct of the police in this scenario.

ETHICS SELF-ASSESSMENT EXERCISES

(There are no strictly right or wrong answers to these exercises. So none is provided. This is to help you put into practice the tests you have be taught in the book on how to make ethical decisions).

SITUATION 1:

Police Officer John does a lawful traffic stop on a 1999 red Honda on Ikorodu Road, seeking to check its papers. He approaches the vehicle and observes a young female driver. The female begins to cry and explain why that she does not have any papers.

Officer John requests to see her papers, but on seeing her crying he gave her a verbal warning for the violation. The female driver is relieved in not being detained, and offers Officer John a card with her name and phone number. She asked him to call her sometime to go out for a drink.

What do you think the officer should do?

SITUATION 2:

Community Police Officer, Andy Taylor, responded to a call about a man walking down Broad Street holding a rifle. Upon arriving at the scene, Officer Taylor determined that the man was not pointing the gun at anyone or acting in a threatening manner. The officer confronted the man, Mr. Femi, who explained that he was walking to the pawnshop on the next block to sell the rifle.

Officer Taylor inquired as to how much money Mr. Femi was looking to get for the rifle, and Femi replied that he was asking $1,000, but would take $800. Officer Taylor knew the rifle was worth far more than that and is considering buying the gun himself. The two men are standing a few feet from an ATM cash machine.

What would be Officer Taylor's wisest course of action?

SITUATION 3:

Detective Jones receives a phone call from Wale, a long-time friend and neighbour who is not in law enforcement. Wale asks Detective Jones for a personal favour. He has just spotted a guy who owes him money driving in the neighbourhood. He was able to get the license plate number and asks Jones to run the registration to find out the owner's address.

Detective Jones knows that this violates department policy, but Wale is a very good friend who has done many favours for Jones over the years. Their families are even planning to vacation together this summer.

What should Jones do?

AN ETHICAL CREED

The World Needs Men and Women

- ➢ Who cannot be bought
- ➢ Whose word is their bond
- ➢ Who put character above wealth
- ➢ Who are larger than their vocations
- ➢ Who do not hesitate to take chances
- ➢ Who will not lose their identity in a crowd
- ➢ Who will be as honest in small things as in great things
- ➢ Who will make not compromises with wrong
- ➢ Whose ambitions are not confined to their own selfish desires
- ➢ Who will not say they do it, "because everyone else does it"
- ➢ Who are true to their friends through good report and evil report, in adversity as well as in prosperity
- ➢ Who do not believe that shrewdness and cunning are the best qualities for winning success

➢ Who are not ashamed to stand for the truth when it is unpopular

➢ Who can say "NO" with emphasis, although the rest of the world is saying "yes"

➢ God make me this kind of person.

By Leonard Wagner

APPENDIX 1

Resolution on Police and Human Rights in Africa

The African Commission on Human and Peoples' Rights (the Commission) meeting at its 54th Ordinary Session, held from 22 October to 5 November 2013 in Banjul, The Gambia,

Recalling its mandate to promote and ensure the protection of human and peoples' rights under the African Charter on Human and Peoples' Rights (the African Charter);

Recognizing the central role of the police in the maintenance and enforcement of law and order and the promotion of citizen's safety as well as the respect for human rights;

Further recognizing the growing demands placed on the police to combat national and transnational crime, terrorism and other emerging security challenges;

Concerned that effective policing in Africa is impeded by several factors including limited financial resources, inadequate training, poor working conditions and corruption;

Further concerned that this situation has led to non-compliance by the police with basic human rights standards in the execution of their duties, including the use of excessive and disproportionate force, extrajudicial killings and summary executions, arbitrary and illegal arrest, torture and mistreatment;

Noting the importance of human rights training for the police as well as efficient mechanisms to follow up on human rights compliance by the police;

Recalling its decision at the 40th and 41st ordinary sessions to organize seminars on Building the Culture of Peace and Human Rights for the Military / Police in Africa;

Reaffirms its commitment to continue to place police and human rights as a priority issue in the execution of its promotion and protection mandate;

Calls on State Parties to the Charter to ensure that in the execution of their duties, police fully comply with the respect for human rights and the rule of law;

Further calls on State Parties to the African Charter to take the appropriate measures in accordance with the relevant Articles of the African Charter and other regional instruments to ensure that police services respect the dignity inherent in the individual in the discharge of their duties.

Done in Banjul, The Gambia, 5 November 2013

APPENDIX 2

Resolution on Police Reform, Accountability and Civilian Police Oversight in Africa[26]

The African Commission on Human and Peoples' Rights at its 40th Ordinary Session held in Banjul, The Gambia, from 15th to 29th November, 2006,

Being aware that police forces throughout Africa play a critical role in the maintenance of law and order, the administration of justice, the respect for the rule of law and enhancing peace and the security of persons and property in every state,

Noting, that policing is increasingly recognized as a basic foundation in building democracy, promoting human and peoples' rights, without which democratic practices, economic, and social development and the promotion of human rights are constrained and even jeopardized,

---

[26] http://www.achpr.org/sessions/40th/resolutions/103a/

Recognizing, that the establishment and existence of many police forces in Africa trace their history from laws and practices which originate from the past colonial experience of our continent,

Concerned that in many of the African States, there exist no independent policing mechanisms, to which members of the public may report police misconduct and abuse of their powers for redress and that where they do, they are directly under the police authorities,

Recognizing that Police forces in African states, which do not have independent oversight mechanisms require reform in order to become effective instruments of security, safety, justice, and respect for human and peoples' rights across the continent,

Further recognizing, that a wealth of local knowledge and experience on policing reform in Africa is available to inform emerging reform initiatives,

Noting that accountability and the oversight mechanisms for policing forms the core of democratic governance and is crucial to enhancing rule of law and assisting in restoring public confidence in police; to develop a culture of human rights, integrity and transparency within the police forces; and to promote a good working relationship between the police and the public at large,

Encouraged by the initiative taken in the formation of the African Policing Civilian Oversight Forum (APCOF), through the collaboration of Civil Society and State Civilian Police Oversight agencies, as an African initiative to promote police reform and with it the building and strengthening of civilian police oversight in Africa,

The African Commission on Human and Peoples' Rights:

1. Calls on State Parties to the African Charter to take measures in terms of Articles 1 and 5 of the African Charter, to ensure that police forces respects the dignity inherent in the individual during the discharge of their duties in the maintenance of law and order;

2. Calls on State Parties to the African Charter to adopt laws and regulations implementing the guidelines contained in the Resolutions of the African Commission on the Guidelines and Measures for the Prohibition and Prevention of Torture, Cruel, Inhuman and Degrading Treatment or Punishment in Africa, otherwise known as the Robben Island Guidelines, as far as they relate to Policing in Africa;

3. Urges State Parties to the African Charter to establish independent civilian policing oversight mechanism, where they do not exist, which shall include civilian participation.

APPENDIX 3

Resolution on the Need to Develop Guidelines on Policing and Assemblies in Africa - ACHPR/Res. 363(LIX) 2016

The African Commission on Human and Peoples' Rights (the Commission), meeting at its 59thOrdinary Session held from 21 October to 4 November 2016 in Banjul, Islamic Republic of The Gambia;

Recalling its mandate to promote and protect human rights in Africa under the African Charter on Human and Peoples' Rights (the African Charter);

Recalling its Guidelines on the Conditions of Arrest, Police Custody and Pre-Trial Detention in Africa andthe Model Law on Access to Information for Africa;

Further recalling its Resolutions ACHPR/Res.103a (XXXX) 06 on Police Reform, Accountability and Civilian Police Oversight in Africa, ACHPR/Res.259 (LIV) 2013 on, Police and Human Rights in Africa, ACHPR/ Res.196 (L) 11 on the Situation of Human Rights Defenders in

Africa, and ACHPR/Res.281 (LV) 2014 on the Right to Peaceful Demonstrations;

Bearing in mind its Resolution ACHPR/Res. 306 (EXT.OS/XVIII) 2015 on the extension of the mandate of the Special Rapporteur on Prisons and Conditions of Detention in Africa which recommends that the Rapporteur should work with other Special Mechanisms of the Commission on cross-cutting issues relating to policing and human rights;

Noting the important role played by the police in ensuring the peaceful conduct of public assemblies and consequently, protecting freedom of expression and assembly;

Mindful of the importance of communication and the right of access to information before, during and after assemblies;

Concerned **by** the persistence of police violence during assemblies in Africa and its apparent consequences on the enjoyment of the various rights enshrined in the African Charter, in particular Articles 4, 5, 6, 9 and 11;

Considering the particularly vulnerable state of human rights defenders and journalists who are more exposed to various forms of police violence during assemblies;

Conscious that in many cases, this situation is caused or aggravated by several factors including the fact that the legal framework does not sufficiently protect the right to freedom of assembly, expression and access to information in the context of public assemblies, the interference of political actors, lack of training for police officers and the non-existence of special mechanisms to monitor policing;

Noting the links between the right to freedom of assembly, freedom of expression and access to information;

Convinced of the urgent need to develop guidelines on policing and assemblies in Africa to guide States Parties to the African Charter, in particular law enforcement officials to ensure greater observance of human rights during assemblies in Africa;

The Commission:
Decides to task the Special Rapporteur on Human Rights Defenders in Africa, the Special Rapporteur on Freedom of Expression and Access to Information in Africa and the Special Rapporteur on Prisons, Conditions of Detention and Policing in Africa to develop the Guidelines on Policing and Assemblies in Africa, including tools to facilitate its effective implementation.

Done in Banjul, Islamic Republic of the Gambia, on 4 November 2016

APPENDIX 4

Launch of the Guidelines on Conditions of Arrest, Police Custody and Pre-Trial Detention in Africa[27]

Held during the 56th Ordinary Session of the African Commission on Human and Peoples' Rights in Banjul, The Gambia from 21 April to 7 May 2015

REPORT

I/INTRODUCTION

The Guidelines on the Conditions of Arrest, Police Custody and Pre-Trial Detention in Africa ('the Luanda Guidelines') were officially launched by the African Commission on Human and Peoples' Rights ('ACHPR') during its 56th Ordinary Session in Banjul, Gambia on 25 April 2015.

The Luanda Guidelines were adopted at the 55th Ordinary Session of the ACHPR in Luanda, Angola in 2014 to provide guidance to policy

---

[27] http://www.achpr.org/news/2015/05/d185

makers and criminal justice practitioners with the aim to strengthen the day-to-day practice of arrest, police custody and pre-trial detention.

The Guidelines are an authoritative interpretation of the African Charter on Human and Peoples' Rights ('the African Charter') and offer specific detail on the measures States Parties to the Charter need to take to uphold, protect and promote the rights of people in the criminal justice system.

Commission Chairperson, Commissioner Zainabo Sylvie Kayitesi, presided over the official launch of the Luanda Guidelines. Formal inputs were provided by, ACHPR Commissioner Med S.K. Kaggwa, ACHPR Commissioner Reine Alapini-Gansou, Niger Police Commissioner Maman Abdel Kader and Ms. Louise Edwards (APCOF).

II/ STATEMENTS FROM THE ACHPR
Commission Chairperson, Commissioner Zainabo Sylvie Kayitesi

The Commission Chairperson welcomed the State delegates and others to the launch, and reiterated the importance of the Luanda Guidelines in promoting a rights-based and African Chartercompliant approach to arrest, police custody and pre-trial detention.

Commissioner Med S.K. Kaggwa

The first formal input was made by Commissioner Med S.K. Kaggwa, who has led the development of the Luanda Guidelines, in his capacity as Special Rapporteur on Prisons and Conditions of Detention in Africa. He recalled that the Guidelines were adopted in response to growing concerns about human rights violations in the pre-trial context across Africa.

Commissioner Kaggwa linked the Guidelines to fundamental rights enshrined in the African Charter, namely the rights to life, liberty, security and a fair trial, noting that many people experience limitations of these rights under current practices.

Commissioner Kaggwa emphasised that working with State Parties, their law enforcement institutions, national human rights institutions and civil society organisations, to implement the Guidelines, is the next important step to improving conditions, procedures and rights of people in pre-trial detention.

Commissioner Kaggwa provided detail on the methodology used in the development of the Guidelines, including reviews by relevant stakeholders at regional consultations held in Banjul, Johannesburg, Nairobi, Dakar and Tunis, as well as written submissions received following the publication of the draft Guidelines on the ACHPR website.

Following a brief summary of the contents of the Guidelines, Commissioner Kaggwa concluded by thanking the African Policing Civilian Oversight Forum ('APCOF'), Danish Institute for Human Rights ('DIHR'), the United Nations Development Programme ('UNDP') and the Open Society Foundations ('OSF') for their technical support, and called on all States to support the Commission's implementation efforts.

Commissioner Reine Alapini-Gansou

Commissioner Alapini-Gansou, the Special Rapporteur on Human Rights Defenders in Africa began by expressing her support for the adoption of the Luanda Guidelines as a strategic working tool, and as another example of how the ACHPR, with its meager resources, strives to give effect to the African Charter.

The Commissioner reiterated earlier comments about the importance of the Luanda Guidelines, given the scale of pre-trial detention in Africa, drawing on a specific example of how the Guidelines could be usefully implemented to promote community-level legal literacy to improve knowledge by people of their rights in the context of arrest, police custody and pre-trial detention.

Commissioner Alapini-Gansou concluded by thanking States and the ACHPR partners, APCOF and DIHR, for their support in the development of the Guidelines.

III/ STATMEMNTS FROM PARTNERS
Louise Edwards, African Policing Civilian Oversight Forum
Ms. Edwards extended her thanks to the ACHPR for providing the space for APCOF, to contribute technical assistance in the development and implementation of the Luanda Guidelines.

She provided statistics on the prevalence of pre-trial detention globally, and in Africa, and raised a number of areas of human rights concerns as a result of the over-use and poor conditions of pre-trial detention on the continent.

Ms. Edwards emphasised the importance of the Luanda Guidelines in providing a blueprint for reform of the entire criminal justice chain, reiterating that all key criminal justice stakeholders, including the police, prison services, judiciary, legal aid providers and oversight mechanisms, have a vital role to play in promoting access to justice and human rights.

She then highlighted three areas where the Luanda Guidelines contribute to the progressive development in international law, namely, discretion to arrest, rights of persons with disabilities, and in articulating an entire accountability architecture for the criminal justice system.

Ms. Edwards concluded by noting that projects to promote implementation of the Guidelines in a number of national contexts were in process, and called on all States and their partners to ensure that the Luanda Guidelines are implemented at the continental, regional and national levels.

Niger Police Commissioner Maman Abdel Kader

Commissioner Kader made his presentation on behalf of the West African Police and Human Rights Platform ('POLI.HR'), an initiative of the National Police Services of Burkina Faso, Niger and Mali which seeks to promote the protection of human rights, and contribute to the work of the ACHPR.

Commissioner Kader commended the ACHPR on the adoption of the Guidelines, and linked what he described as an important development by the Commission to the vital work that police organisations do at the regional and national levels, to promote a rights-based approach to arrest and custody. He noted the opportunities for the ACHPR and POLI.HR to collaborate on the implementation of the Guidelines in Burkina Faso, Niger and Mali.

Specifically, Commissioner Kader pointed to the utility of the Guidelines in basic and in-service training, in monitoring places of detention, and in relation to the collection and dissemination of statistical data on arrest and persons in police custody.

Commissioner Kader also emphasised the role that platforms such as POLI.HR can play in sensitising the ACHPR to the policing terrain at the sub-regional and national level, which can assist the ACHPR in finessing its implementation work with police organisations.

The Commissioner concluded by offering POLI.HR's expertise to the ACHPR in the implementation of the Guidelines.

IV/OFFICIAL LAUNCH
Following the formal presentations from the panel, the Guidelines were officially launched.

RELATED BOOKS BY DR OMOLE

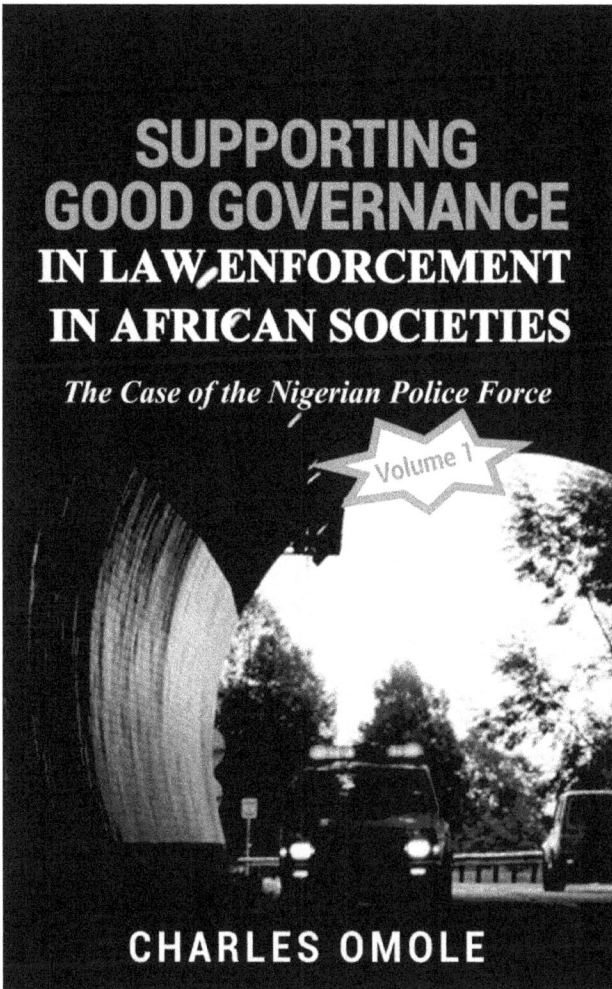

SUPPORTING GOOD GOVERNANCE
IN LAW ENFORCEMENT
IN AFRICAN SOCIETIES

The Case of the Nigerian Police Force

Volume 1

CHARLES OMOLE

Contact Information for Dr Charles Omole

Charlesomole@Gmail.com